MW01104962

FriesenPress

Suite 300 - 990 Fort St
Victoria, BC, V8V 3K2
Canada

www.friesenpress.com

Copyright © 2019 by Alyse Bukach
First Edition — 2019

ISBN
978-1-5255-3869-8 (Hardcover)
978-1-5255-3870-4 (Paperback)
978-1-5255-3871-1 (eBook)

1. POETRY

Distributed to the trade by The Ingram Book Company

My Treasured Moments

Alyse Bukach

Acknowledgments

I want to thank my loving husband, Richard, for putting up with long days/nights of frustration for months on end. I am grateful for his support; he always encourages me to keep going. Most of all, I thank him for enduring the long roads of my health issues with me.

I thank my parents, Allan and Donna, my daughter Rachel and her family, cousin Karla, sister-in-law Rosemarie, best friend Robin, and all my other family and friends. I appreciate their support with getting me through the ups and downs of being a writer and with dealing with my deafness as well as other health problems.

I thank Carrie Aulenbacher, who artistically created my website www.alysebukachauthors.com, and Cher Duncombe, who always provided encouragement. They both gave me advice and support—valuable tools that aided me to accomplish my dreams and adventures.

I thank Heather Pendley (PendleysProEditing.com) for editing my book. She did a wonderful job, which was well above and beyond what I was expecting. She is detail-oriented, with an eye for words. I highly recommend Heather to anyone.

I thank everyone at FriesenPress for all their help to get my first book published.

The cover art of my book is made with a scarf from the 1940's and a wood chest from the 1970's, both of which were owned by my dear mother-in-law Rose Bukach.

R.I.P. Rose Bukach
Nov 25, 1921 to Mar 15, 2018

Spiritual

Mystical Sapphire–Blue Ocean

I'm transported into the most mystical place of warmth and soothing sounds that I could ever imagine. Sitting back and closing my eyes, I listen to what's all around me. A gentle breeze carries the unmistakable scent of the ocean as the sunlight sprinkles the moving waters with crystals of light. A profound sense of relaxation washes over me, and I enjoy the wondrous feeling of peace and tranquility. The mysterious colours are ever changing from the deepest blue to palest aqua. It invokes my fantasies of sun-kissed lagoons and crystal-clear pools hidden by lush foliage. As my mind and body go into an energizing sensation of complete well-being, I drift off into a relaxing dreamland. As I come around from my dream, I get the sense that there are sea creatures about. I look out towards the middle of the blue ocean and concentrate on what is out there—is it a dolphin, an orca? Or could it be just the waves moving about?

The mystical, sapphire-blue ocean speaks to all sea creatures and mammals to let them know what Mother Nature's plans are. The blue ocean can be a beautiful but dangerous place to live for animals and people, too.

The mystical, sapphire-blue ocean can change from night to day, day to night, as do all my writing patterns.

From adventures, dreams, and true-life experiences, to spiritual experiences, past, present, and future.

Whispers from Above
June 2018

Whispers in the air are dreams searching for a home,
dreams of wild imaginings for you and you alone.
Gently kissed on the breeze, when silently approaching,
whisper to your doubting heart sweet, never-end-
    ing hope.
So, when the wind is calling, and your heart is touched
    with love,
reach out for the special dreams that come from
    up above.
When whisperings you hear no more and silence fills
    your breast,
you'll know that dreams you've longed for have finally
    come to rest.
So, when others search for a dream to be their own
tell them: listen to the whispers in the air—your dream is
    coming home.

Believe in Spirituality
May 2017

Spirituality is a brave search for the truth about existence
and requires fearlessly peering into the mysterious
nature of life.

When you realize that other dimensions exist, you'll
never think of life, death, yourself, or the universe in
the same way again.

The spiritual life does not remove us from the world, but
leads us deeper into it.

Believe in Yourself
October 2002

I believe in miracles and dreams that will come true
I believe in tender moments and friendship, through
    and through.
I believe in stardust and moonbeams all aglow
I believe there's magic, and more than we can ever know.

I believe in reaching out and touching from the heart
I believe that if we touch another person's heart, it's a gift.
I believe that if you cry, your tears are not in vain
When you're sad and lonely, others know your pain.
I believe that when we laugh, a sparkle starts to shine
I know that spark will spread from more hearts
    than mine.

I believe that hidden in the quiet night there are magic,
    gypsies, dragons, and spirits.
I believe that if you dance the dances of your heart
greater happiness will find a new way to start.

I believe the gifts you have are there for you to share,
and when you give them from your heart, the whole world
    knows deep down you care.
I believe that if you give, even just to one
that gift will grow in magnitude before the day is done.

I believe that comfort comes from giving part of me
If I share with others, there's more for all to see.
I believe that love is still the greatest gift of all
and when it's given from the heart, then not one of us
will fall.

Living with Deafness

The Paintbrush
1999

I keep my paintbrush with me, wherever I may go
in case I need to cover up, so the Real Me doesn't show.
I'm so afraid to show you Me, afraid of what you'll do
you might laugh or say mean things
I'm afraid I might lose you.
I'd like to remove all my paint coats to show you the real,
    true Me
but I want you to understand, I need you to like what
    you see.
So, if you'll be patient and close your eyes, I'll strip off my
    coats real slow.
Please understand how much it hurts to let the Real
    Me show.
Now my coats are stripped off, I feel naked, bare and cold.
If you still love Me with all you see, you're my friend, pure
    as gold.
I need to save my paintbrush, though, and hold it in
    my hand;
I want to keep it close to me, in case you can't understand.
So please protect me, my dear friend, and thanks for
    loving Me so true
but please let me keep my paintbrush
until I love Me, too!

The Experiences
July 2010

For only each one of us knows our own personal thoughts
our unique past and personal history
the experiences that brought us to the crossroads we
    now face.
We can always learn at least a small degree from
    others' experiences,
and yet no one else can walk in our shoes.
Others know not the trials and tribulations faced
    in private
for each is individual, unique, and personal.
And that is why, while standing at the crossroads
only we can formulate decisions for ourselves.
The true direction that lies within
the choices we must deliberate on with clarity
    and wisdom.
For it is only through personal reflection
that we can now choose our destiny
our next adventure
and the future we will embrace.

Our Long Roads Travelled

Jan 2010

I cannot speak for all who stem
long roads less travelled their way
nor question choices made by them
in days long past or nights long dim
by words they spoke and did not say.
Each road is long, though short it seems
and credence gives each road a name
of fantasies, sun-drenched in beams
or choices turned to darkened dreams
to where each road wends just the same.
From north to south, then back again,
we follow birds like all the rest.
Escaping nature's snowy den
on roads we've seen and places been
forsaking roads that travelled west.
This journey grows now to its end
as road reflections lined in chrome
give way to roads with greater bend
an empty sign that still pretends
It points the way to our home sweet home.
But all roads lead to where we go
and where we go is where we've been

so, home is just a word we know
that space in time most appropriate
for where we want to be again.
For even home, it seems to me, is still a choice we all
    must face
from day to day, we endlessly choose
if a home is going to be another road or just a place.

Imagine Being Deaf
2013

Imagine being deaf
to your soul mate.
To never hear
your lover's words
of promise and adoration.
To never hear those words
"I love you"
resonate and fill you with
that joy of ages.
Imagine to be deaf
to your peers.
To never hear
their complaints about
your appearance and attitude.
To never hear those words,
"You're an idiot"
clang about and wound
your spirit.
Imagine being deaf
to your family.
To never hear
your parents' words
of encouragement and praise.
To never hear your grandchildren's voices,

never hear your friends.
To never hear those words,
"We love you"
flow in ease and
help you sleep at night.
Imagine to be deaf
to the world.
To never hear
wildlife, thunderstorms, rain.
To never hear those words,
"Please help us"
drag you into our pit
of guilt and sin.
Imagine to be deaf
to your peers,
And to the world.
Imagine being deaf
to all things.
To never hear
the pain or joy
that follows our speech.
To never have that feeling
of acceptance in the world.
And to always miss
those vital moments.

A New Language for Me

December 2012

Try to learn a new language—it's not very easy to do
I need your help and assistance,
so I thought I'd explain it to you.
Next time you are going to speak to me
don't turn your head away
for only by seeing the words on your lips
can I understand what you say.
Talk to me more distinctly: not too loud and not too fast.
Don't hide your lips behind a cup or your hand
or keep talking when you're walking past.
When you patiently say "never mind" I shiver up inside
for I frantically fought to hear what was said,
you don't know how hard I tried.
The tick of a clock, the sound of a bird
the sound on the roof of the rain.
Approaching footsteps, a loved one's voice,
what I'd give to hear them again.
Please help me remember
through the picture of a word,
a sound, a melody that once I loved
and that once I also heard.

A Father's Love
2000

Children hardly know or guess
the love their father can't express.
With thoughts he seldom says aloud
his heart is warm, his feeling proud.
They do not fully understand
his wisdom and his guiding hand.
They do not know each helpful word
holds love unspoken, love unheard.
Yet as the busy years roll past,
they come to understand at last.
The worries and the fears he knew
the problem times he pulled them through.
They finally learn the full extent
of what a father's love has meant
And realize how great it's been
to have a father just like him

Love
1997

Love is the light and sunshine of life; we cannot fully enjoy ourselves or anything unless someone we love enjoys it with us. Even if we are alone, we store up our enjoyment, in hope of sharing it later with those we love.

My Love for You
1996

My love for you is something rare,
strong and vibrant like mountain air.
And yet it's like the valley's flow,
deep and quiet with winter snow.
My love for you is filled with grace
deeply woven like snowflakes' lace.
Gently falling upon the ground
like silent magic, it's so profound.
My love for you is heaven blue
with winter's clouds passing through.
Filled with tears of ice and snow
that brings a joy you'll never know.

Parents' Love

Dedicated to my parents Allan & Donna.
June 2012

We never know or fully realize
how sweet and kind our parents are
how gentle and how wise.
We simply take for granted
from day to passing day
each sacrifice they make for us
in their own loving way.
But then we grow and finally learn
the way that children do
how much their love has really meant,
how thoughtful they've been to us
and so this comes with all our thanks.
You both deserve it and more
for there aren't two dearer parents
than the one this poem is for.
I love you both with all my heart
Mom and Dad

Treasures
June 24, 2012

Your love is a fire, consuming my heart in its flame
a fire burning wild and free, so difficult to tame.
You easily seduce me with the sound of your voice
no matter how I feel, I really have no choice.
Whispering sweet words as your fingers touch my skin
with a kiss from your lips, let the love-making begin.
Only you know how to give me this pleasure
The times we make love are the moments I treasure.

The One in the Glass
1995

When you get what you want in your struggles for self
and the world makes you king for a day
just go to a mirror and look at yourself
and see what that person has to say.
For it isn't your father or mother or spouse
whose judgement upon you must pass,
the person whose verdict counts most in your life
is the one staring back from the glass.
Some people might think you're a straight shootin' chum
and call you a wonderful gal or guy,
but the person in the glass says you're only a bum
if you can't look yourself in the eye.
You're the one to please, never mind all the rest
for you're with yourself clear to the end,
and you've passed one of life's most dangerous tests
if the person in the glass is your friend.
You may fool the whole world down the pathway of years
and get pats on your back as you pass,
but your final reward will be heartache and tears
if you've cheated the one in the glass.

My Feelings Toward You
Dedicated to my loving Richard
2013

Every time I'm with you,
there's a constant smile on my face.
The piece missing from my heart,
you have somehow replaced.
You know that I care about you, Richard
but you don't know how much.
I find myself falling in love,
with someone I feel I can trust.
I love it when you hold me,
and look into my eyes.

I love to feel your body,
when it's pressed against mine.
I constantly have butterflies in my stomach,
and I can hardly speak.
My heart is always pounding so fast,
my knees feel so weak.
Even though I do not know much,
I think that I have finally found,
the one who I will always be with.
'Til God takes me away,
I want to tell you this.
How I really feel,

but I find it hard to admit,
that this is all so real.

The love that we share now,
will be holding our future together.
I want to let you know firsthand,
Richard, I'm making plans.
All it involves is me and you,
and it all started when you and I,
fell in love with each other.

Dreams

Death Becomes Me
September 1993, Vulcan, Alberta

Twelve miles out on our farm, east of town. As I sit on my porch, I look out across the pasture in the night air. The moon is full and the sky is bright with stars. There's a gentle breeze going through my hair. It's half past midnight, and I am wondering what to do. A strange feeling runs through me as I walk down a path that wasn't there before. At the end of the path is a spooky-looking graveyard, but it seems peaceful there. As I walk through the gates, the air gets stale and still. Fear surrounds me.

Looking around, I sense the undead is alive tonight. Vampires, werewolves, witches, and zombies seem to fill the emptiness around me. I look to the right, then to the left, and see nothing, but I feel a breath of cool air running down my spine. As I turn around, what do I see? The Reaper. Is he here for me? His boney hand stretches out to me as if I'm to hold it. As I look at him, peace washes over me.

But the question is: Do I go with him? What does that mean—have I died? No, it can't be: I can't be dead. As I try to walk away, a strange sense of love, without pain, settles within me. I see a bright light in the distance. It radiates comfort and love. It tells me to follow. From inside the Reaper's dark cape, his boney hand waves for me to follow.

The Reaper is walking towards the light telling me, "We must go now."

Something tells me to follow, but if I go, what will happen? As I get closer to the light, I hear voices of people I seem to recognize, voices of people who I haven't seen in a long time, friends or relatives who have passed away. What's happening to me? I look around and start to see things that make me shiver all over. I want to run, but on the other hand, I see things that make me want to stay.

What am I going to do? As I look towards the Reaper I shake my head, for I want to stay. *I have things to live for.*

Thinking this, I start backing away from the bright light and the Reaper. As he turns to look at me, I get a glimpse inside the dark cape; he's telling me I can't go back. The time has come for me to take on another life, a life of peacefulness without pain. But no, I have to go back. I try to say, "I have to live my life with my children," but voices coming from the light get louder. I scream for help, no one seems to hear me. I beg for mercy and to let me go back. I will change for the better, not worse. As I back up, I run into something cold and hard. I turn to look, and behold, it's a gravestone. I read what is written—my name! I scream for mercy again. The Reaper moves closer to me, and as he touches me, a strange feeling comes over me. Forgiveness courses through me, a strange tingling runs through my body, warmth and love enfolds me.

What happened? Had I died? No, but I was forgiven. Until the next time.

Who Am I?
2014

Being a woman of almost 50,
I wonder who I am.
Taking a look at my life in the past,
gives me a glance of who I've been.
I wonder if I'm as good as I was back then.
I live my life the best I can,
but I still wonder who the hell I really am.
I saw the light one stormy night,
it made me see what I could write.

Thinking of You

By Derice Layher and Alyse Bukach
1996

When I think of you,
I think of smiling, laughing,
because you always make me smile.
When I try to think of anything else,
thoughts of you surface, unbidden.
Something you said, something you did,
and I'm lost in thoughts of seeing you sad,
confused.
It seems so out of place, so foreign
that it hurts.
I want to say something, do something,
anything
to make the confusion go away
and to make you smile.
But knowing I can't makes it so much harder
to keep you out of my mind and my heart.

Personal Feelings

Warrior of Pain
1998

My pain is like a ball, sometimes round, and some-
    times small
on a good day you can laugh and smile.
You can dance and you can sing.
You can dine with friends, if only for a short while.
But when the Pain arrives, it's all together another thing.
Sometimes the pain creeps up slowly,
little warning does it give.
For-the fury that is on its way,
a burden thrust upon me.
Requiring so much strength just to live.
The pain is now not so small,
nor is it like a round, small ball.
The pain is as hot as the colour red,
and spreads spasmodically
with each and every breath.
"No," I tell my doctor, who doesn't listen to me,
this pain is not just a figment of my imagination
nor something that I have manifested or created
like a story in my head.
My pain is in my pelvis, affecting all that lies within.
I brace for the electric shocks, the muscle spasms
and the excruciating pain when I feel like I am
    being stabbed

repeatedly with sharp, red-hot pins and needles.
My pain does not allow me the privilege of sitting
nor working, nor socializing at length
because at its worst, it drains me of my composure
and of every last bit of my strength.
But my dearest Pain, there is something you should know
I am strong, I am determined and through these tears
    you'll see me fight.
I am young, I am proud and I will once again shine
because my dearest, Pain,
I will not and I shall not
allow you to dim my light!
Within myself I am a warrior
who will continue on

Alberta Storms
1999/2000

The rushing of the wind, sweet smells in the air.
The menace of the dark clouds in the evening sky,
I witness from my home, as the world sets on fire.
And Thor's mighty blows from the heavens fly.

Sharp zig-zagging lightning flashes,
Bright and eerie, far and wide.
Claps of thunder threaten briefly,
dancing down the mountain side.
This is one of my Alberta storms,
only one of my Alberta storms.

The colours blowing round make my hair stand on end,
the feeling that my spirit's growing in my soul.
Our bodies weaving love, as angels cry in joy,
the moment of the union is our only goal.

Sharp zig-zagging lightning flashes,
bright and weary, far and wide.
Claps of thunder threaten briefly,
dancing down my lover's side.
This is one of my Alberta storms,
another one of my Alberta storms.

Let Me Be Blonde
Dedicated to my daughter Rachel
1998

Tired and downhearted,
you simply want a break.
From troubles and woes,
and life's little blows.
Then this is the step to take,
Please
let me be blonde,
let me be free of all worldly cares.
Like thinking affairs and hiring au pairs,
just let me rejoice in come hither stares.
Brunettes are intellectual,
redheads have a flair.
But being blonde makes everyone,
think your head is full of air.

Assumptions that you're silly,
dizzy, stupid, and dumb.
When you're blonde you don't know,
your finger from your thumb.
Please
let me be blonde,
let me be free of all worldly cares.
Like thinking affairs and hiring au pairs,

just let me rejoice in come-hither stares.
Dyed or real, true-blue or fake,
being blonde is what it takes.

Inspiration-Less Blues
1998/1999

When I put my pen to paper, nothing comes to mind.
I search the dictionary, but there're no words I can find.
My muse has come up empty, my rhyming's gone to bed.
I hope and dream and struggle and scream,
no poetry's in my head.
I got the
Absolutely,
inspiration-less blues.
Don't want to be creative, I only want to eat.
Don't give me education, just give me something sweet.
I'm standing at the crossroads,
Don't know which way to go.
My life, my arts and bodily parts,
were struck a mortal blow.

I got the
Absolutely,
inspiration-less blues.
I got the
Absolutely,
confused in my ever-loving heart.
Inspiration-less blues,
Don't ask me to write anything more, 'cause it just ain't
    gonna happen.

Got the Blues

Dedicated to the ones I've lost
between these years.
Always and forever in my heart
2000/2003

It's a sunny weekend morning,
and all the folks around me.
For some reason, look so happy.
I'm just getting through my first coffee,
after an all-night jam party.
So now, honey, I'm gonna tell you.
I know one day you'll wake up,
and you'll be feeling so lonely.
You'll know like I do now,
you've got the blues.
They're come to break you down.
You know, I gave you all I could,
but I guess you had it figured.
I didn't have quite enough to give,
So, I think you had your choice, man.
I'd have to break my back, or you could break my heart.
Still, I miss you so much, man.

I sometimes can't sleep at night,
can't stop reaching for you.
I got the blues, they've come to break me down.

When I get to go home tonight,
I see your picture on the wall.
Looking down at me with your smile,
I remember the way you looked.
When you walked out that door the very last time,
I wish you would come back to me.
Maybe we could start our love all over,
make it happen, make it right.
But I know that you don't want me,
I got the blues, they've come to break me down.
Yeah, those blues, when they get you,
they twist your soul and leave you crying.
And the entire world seems to change,
to hard stone, and cold, cold ice, but you know it when
    you feel it.

You've got the blues, they've come to break you down.
You know, you have to wear a brave face,
don't want nobody to see.
The pain in your heart, or tears in your eyes.
Still they know, 'cause you can't really hide it.
You've got the blues, they've come to break you down.

Grief

You and I Are Blind

2010

You and me, we are star-stuff.
The stuff of which the universe was made billions of
     years ago.
The stuff of the trees, flowers, rivers, and lakes.
The stuff of oceans deep, mysterious mountains
     of granite,
Silver, gold, sapphires, and gems.
We are all that. No less
You and me, we are star-stuff.
Born of the microcosmic essence of the infinite universe,
Together we are one with God, brilliant, ancient, ever-
     lasting star.
We are all that! No less
We look ahead, look behind,
Look around for you shall find.
Who now is talking but the voice of your mind?
Do you not know?
Do you not see?
How I am you and you are me?
The pain you cause to others,
They did not suffer, for they could not suffer.

As they are you and you are me.
Though you have learned the lesson of truth, others have
    yet to see.
That the ones they hurt are you and me.
So to you, I give this gift,
The gift of light and love.
Do not hurt others as you have before.
If you do, their pain will be at your door,
For they are you and you are me.
We are one now, can't you see?
Walk with me on my journey, for it is yours as well
    as mine.
Come on, come with me, we both shall be fine.
Look at the sun, how brightly she shines on our path,
She shines for you and for me.
Look how she laughs, she laughs so hard for she is happy
    as can be.
For she knows the likes of you and me.
Come with me to the rock and rest awhile.
Can't you see the beautiful view?
It is there for me and for you.
No, please don't be still and rest.
Don't act like such a pest,
I told you once, I told you twice.
And I will not tell you thrice.

Fine, if that's the way it is, you sadden me.
Go on your own, I may see you along the way.
Now I'm all alone and sad, for how can I be glad?
My friend had abandoned me,

But in my sadness, I sit and see.
The truth of it all, of you and me.
It is a beautiful vision for any to behold,
Although you may have to be bold.
Can't you see? Can't you see?
The pain you've caused to you and to me?
Now the vision is done and the lesson learnt.
Don't you understand? I did not get my fingers burnt,
Although you may be feeling pain.
It is not real, it is not real.
Look at the people, how you helped them be free.
Can't you see it was destined to be?
That you would have to leave me?

Now you know the truth, but you still can't see.
For you are blind to the wonder of me.
Do not cry, do not fear.
Your story is the best that I hear .
Do you see, do you see?
The lesson has been learnt for you and me,
Do you know
how you glow
with the light of love that was given?
To you, from me

Dear Rose

Dedicated to my mother-in-law,
Rose Bukach. R.I.P
March 15, 2018

You are the mother I received the day I wed your son,
and I want to thank you, Mom, for the loving things
     you've done.
You've given me a gracious man with whom I share
     my life.
You are his lovely mother and I, his lucky wife.
You used to pat his little head and now I hold his hand.
You raised in love a little boy and gave to me a man.
In a bittersweet moment, another angel has found
     her wings,
and has set off on her flight.
Safe into the arms of God, to those gone before her.
Waiting and anticipating her arrival,
as Rose makes her way into heaven.
We can shed tears that Rose is gone,
or we can smile because she has lived.
We can close our eyes and pray that Rose will come back,
or we can open our eyes and see all that Rose has left.
Our hearts can be empty because we can't see her,
or we can be full of the love that we shared.
We can turn our backs on tomorrow and live in yesterday,
or we can be happy for tomorrow because of yesterday.

We all can remember Rose and that she is gone,
or we can cherish Rose's memory and let it live on.
We can cry and close our minds, be empty and turn
    our backs,
or we can do what Rose, Baba, Mom would have wanted:
Smile, open our eyes, love, and go on.

About the Author

Alyse M. Bukach was born in 1968 in Calgary, Alberta, Canada. She currently calls Athabasca, Alberta home. She and her loving husband, Richard, enjoy the beautiful country full-time in their fifth wheel trailer. She gives guidance and help to others through her words, for it is only through personal reflections that we can choose our destiny and embrace our next adventure. She realizes that her deafness and Chronic Pain Disorder are never going away, but she uses positive thoughts to inspire and motivate herself to continue on her journey. Being with loved ones, taking pictures, and writing are what she loves best.

Learn more about Alyse at:
www.alysebukachauthors.com

CPSIA information can be obtained
at www.ICGtesting.com
Printed in the USA
LVHW091906040819
626477LV00003B/4/P

9 781525 538698